IMAGES OF WAR

BATTLE OF KURSK 1943

RARE PHOTOGRAPHS FROM WARTIME ARCHIVES

Hans Seidler

Pen & Sword
MILITARY

First published in Great Britain in 2011 by
PEN & SWORD MILITARY
An imprint of
Pen & Sword Books Ltd
47 Church Street
Barnsley
South Yorkshire
S70 2AS

ISBN 978-1-84884-393-6

Typeset by Concept, Huddersfield, West Yorkshire
Printed and bound in England by CPI UK

Pen & Sword Books Ltd incorporates the imprints of Pen & Sword Aviation, Pen & Sword Maritime, Pen & Sword Military, Wharncliffe Local History, Pen & Sword Select, Pen & Sword Military Classics, Leo Cooper, Remember When, Seaforth Publishing and Frontline Publishing.

For a complete list of Pen & Sword titles please contact
PEN & SWORD BOOKS LIMITED
47 Church Street, Barnsley, South Yorkshire, S70 2AS, England
E-mail: enquiries@pen-and-sword.co.uk
Website: www.pen-and-sword.co.uk

Contents

Assessment of the German Soldier in 1943

For the German soldier on the Eastern Front the opening months of 1943 were gloomy. He had fought desperately to maintain cohesion and hold positions that often saw thousands perish. By May 1943 the German forces were holding a battle line more than 1,400 miles in overall length, which had been severely weakened by the overwhelming strength of the Red Army. To make matters worse, during the first half of 1943, many troop units lacked proper replacements to compensate for the large losses sustained. Supplies of equipment and ammunition were also becoming insufficient in some areas of the front. Many soldiers had become aware that if they did not stem the Russian onslaught they would soon find themselves in dire circumstances. As a result, in a number of sectors of the front, soldiers were able to form a realistic assessment of the war situation, and this in turn managed to save the lives of many who might otherwise have died fighting to the last man.

In spite of the adverse situation in which the German soldier was placed during the first half of 1943, many remained steadfast, especially in Army Group Centre, and determined to fight with courage and skill. By June 1943 the German soldier had expended considerable combat efforts lacking sufficient reconnaissance and the necessary support of tanks and heavy weapons to ensure any type of success. The Red Army had constantly outgunned them, and the *Luftwaffe* air support was almost non-existent in a number of areas of the front. The short summer nights too had caused considerable problems for the men, for they only had a few hours of darkness in which to conceal their night marches and construction of field fortifications. Ultimately, the German soldier in the summer of 1943 was ill prepared to launch a massive offensive in the East, even with the considerable support of the *Panzerwaffe*. Commanders in the field were fully aware of the significant problems and the difficulties imposed by underequipped soldiers to fight in any large operation. However, in the end they had no other choice than to order their troops to fight with whatever they had at their disposal.

Chapter One

Preparations for Battle

The history of the Battle of Kursk began with the German Army Group Centre during the summer of 1941 when on 22 June, the German Army, 3,000,000 strong, began their greatest attack in military history. In Army Group Centre, under the command of Field Marshal Fedor von Bock, 800 Panzers struck across the Russian frontier and within hours the German armoured punch, with brilliant co-ordination of all arms, had pulverised bewildered Russian formations. With nothing but a string of victories behind them by the end of September 1941, Army Group Centre was regrouped for the final assault on Moscow, known as 'Operation Typhoon'. At first the drive to Moscow went well, but by early October the weather began to change as cold driving rain fell on the troops. Within hours the Russian countryside had been turned into a quagmire with roads and fields becoming virtually impassable. All roads leading to Moscow had become a boggy swamp. To make matters worse, since 'Typhoon' had began, Army Group Centre had lost nearly 35,000 men, excluding the sick and injured; some 240 tanks and heavy artillery pieces; and over 800 other vehicles that had either developed mechanical problems or had been destroyed. Supplies were becoming dangerously low, and fuel and ammunition were hardly adequate to meet the ever-growing demands of the drive to Moscow. Regardless of the dwindling shortages of material, Army Group Centre was ordered to continue its march through the freezing arctic conditions. Despair now gripped the front as battered and exhausted troops froze to death in front of the Russian capital. Its territorial gains that winter were limited to a forty-mile belt at the approach to Moscow.

The failure to capture Moscow had been a complete disaster for Army Group Centre. Its forces had altered out of recognition from those of its victorious summer operations. But during early 1942 the Russian offensive petered out. The temperatures rose and Army Group Centre began to replenish its losses. June 1942 saw the preparation of another German summer offensive. However, instead of attacking Moscow again, Army Group Centre consolidated its positions, while Army Group South advanced to the Caucasus and the Volga. Then, as the battle of Stalingrad raged in the ruins of the city, a major Soviet offensive in the Moscow area was unleashed, code-named 'Operation Mars'. The objective was to destroy the Rzhev salient.

Already Army Group Centre had heavily fortified the salient with a mass of mine belts, trenches, bunkers, anti-tank guns and machine gun emplacements. A well constructed road network allowed the rapid movement of reinforcements to the area. The Russian offensive failed with heavy casualties. However, three months later in February 1943 the strong lines of defences of Army Group Centre were yet again attacked. The Russians made a co-ordinated assault in the Kursk and northern Army Group Centre areas with the ultimate objective of encircling the Army Group. But yet again the Red Army over estimated the strength and resilience of the German forces in Army Group Centre and eventually the Soviet attacks from Kursk towards Orel failed to make progress. As a result the offensive was called off.

Throughout the first half of 1943 Army Group Centre had more or less maintained the strategic initiative on the Eastern Front, and it was for this prime reason that Hitler was confronted with a tempting strategic opportunity that he was convinced would yield him victory. This victory, he thought, would be undertaken at a place called Kursk, and it would prove to be the last great German offensive on the Eastern Front. The attack would be launched against a huge Russian salient at Kursk measuring some 120 miles wide and 75 miles deep.

At his Eastern Front headquarters, Wolf's Lair, Hitler tried for hours to persuade his commanders that his force could attack from north and south of the salient in a huge pincer movement and encircle the Red Army. In Hitler's view, the offensive would be the greatest armoured battle ever won on the Eastern Front and would include the bulk of his mighty *Panzerwaffe*, among them his elite *Waffen SS* divisions.

However, as usual, Hitler ignored the true capabilities of the Red Army at Kursk. The Soviets not only outnumbered their opponents by approximately 2.5 to 1, they also exceeded the Germans in guns and tanks. Their defences too were manned in special defensive regions and belts, anti-tank strong points, and an extensive network of engineer obstacles. The strength of the Soviet defences at Kursk varied considerably. Where it was expected that the main attacks would take place, Red Army commanders concentrated the largest number of defenders on the narrowest frontages. Unbeknown to the German planners, on the Russian Front at Kursk there were some 870 soldiers, 4.7 tanks, and 19.8 guns and mortars to every mile of defensive front. However, just prior to the German attack, as more intelligence was gathered on the coming battle, this density would increase to more than 4,500 troops, forty-five tanks, and 104.3 guns per mile. On the Voronezh Front, where it was particularly weaker, about 2,500 men, forty-two tanks, and fifty-nine guns and mortars were fielded in every mile of the sector. In total the Voronezh Front contained some 573,195 soldiers, 8,510 guns and mortars, and 1,639 tanks and self-propelled guns. Both the Central and Voronezh Fronts alone contained more than 1,300,000 men, 19,794 artillery pieces and mortars, 3,489 tanks and self-propelled guns, and some 2,650 aircraft. Behind this fearsome force stood additional troops of the Steppe Front. Although only 295,000 of Steppe Front men, including 900 tanks, would be moved forward during the battle, they had additional resources to commit another 200,000 men and another 600 tanks. The total number of men available in the Red Army at Kursk was 1,910,361, including 5,040 tanks. This was a very impressive array of military might. With such a high concentration of men and weapons, the Red Army undoubtedly had overall superiority and exceeded the Germans in men, tanks and guns.

Despite Hitler's confidence, many of the German generals were not blind to the difficulties facing them at Kursk. In fact, a number of them were concerned at the enemy's growing strength. But it was not until they unleashed their forces against the Red Army that even they finally realised how far they had underestimated the grand scale of their enemy's defences and the massive forces assembled against them.

By June 1943, German plans for the battle at Kursk were finally issued to all the commanders in the field. The code name for the attack was called Operation 'Citadel' or 'Zitadelle'. The plan was for the German forces to smash Red Army formations and leave the road to Moscow open. For this daring offensive, the German force was distributed between the Northern and Southern groups, consisting of a total of twenty-two divisions, six of which were Panzer and five *Panzergrenadier*. The main attack fell to the 9th Army in the north. There were some 335,000 soldiers, 590 tanks and 424 assault guns. In the south, the Germans fielded a much stronger force and concentrated 349,907 troops, 1,269 tanks and 245 assault guns.

Putting together such a strong force was a great achievement, but the *Panzerwaffe* of 1943 were unlike those armoured forces that had victoriously steamrolled across western Russia two years earlier. The losses during the previous winter had resulted in the drastic reductions in troop strength. Despite the *Panzerwaffe*'s impressive array of firepower, this shortage of infantry was to lead to Panzer units being required to take on more ambitious tasks normally preserved for the infantry. To make matters worse the *Panzerwaffe* were facing an even greater enemy, coupled with almost impregnable defensive belts.

Already, within weeks of the attack, the Russians had constructed more than six major defensive belts, each subdivided into two or even three layers of well-defended strongholds. The first two belts were occupied by forward troops, while units that were held in reserve occupied the third and fourth belts. The last two belts were virtually empty of soldiers and used mainly to accommodate reserves if the need arose. Each belt was a maze of intricate blockhouses and trenches. In some areas of the belt the Russians had emplaced more than 70,000 anti-tank and 64,000 anti-personnel mines.

In front of the Soviet defensive fortress stood the cream of all the German combat formations at Kursk, the premier divisions of the *Waffen SS*. In Army South these elite soldiers were deployed for action, ready at a moment's notice to fight their way through the formidable lines of barbed wire entanglements, mine fields and anti-tank guns. Here, the *II.SS-Panzerkorps*, commanded by *SS-Obergruppenführer* Paul Hausser, formed part of the *4.Panzerarmee*. The corps comprised the three elite *Waffen SS* divisions, the *1.SS-Panzerdivision 'Leibstandarte Adolf Hitler'*, the *2.SS-Panzerdivision 'Das Reich'* and the *3.SS-Panzerdivision 'Totenkopf'*. These three divisions had a line strength of 390 of the latest tanks and 104 assault guns between them, including forty-two of the Army Group's *Tiger* tanks. At their starting positions, the three *SS* divisions covered a sector that was 12 miles wide. The *'Totenkopf'* occupied the left flank of the advance, the *'Leibstandarte'* was in the centre and *'Das Reich'* held the right. It was hoped that these *Waffen SS* divisions would play a decisive part in the victory at Kursk.

For the next few weeks prior to the battle both the Soviets and their German counter parts were increasingly tense as the offensive ominously approached. Although there was almost a feeling of self doubt within the ranks of the Red Army, especially as no force had ever halted a deliberate *Blitzkrieg* offensive before, each soldier must have been comforted by the belief in their readiness and the great labyrinth of defensive positions that covered hundreds of square miles in front of their opponents.

During early July 1943, neither side got much rest. Russian soldiers, after months of preparation, were waiting and ready, sitting in their bunkers and numerous other well dug-in positions for the first sign of attack. The final showdown on the Eastern Front was about to begin.

June or July 1943, and German troops are seen relaxing and drinking prior to the Kursk offensive. As the date for the battle approached neither side got much rest. In front of the German positions Russian soldiers, after months of preparation, were waiting and ready, sitting in their bunkers and numerous other well dug-in positions for the first sign of attack.

An 8.14cm GrW 34 mortar crew prior to the opening attack in a dugout. A shelter quarter not only protects the weapon from dust and rain, but also helps to camouflage it from aerial surveillance. During the war the mortar had become the standard infantry company support weapon giving the soldier valuable high explosive capability beyond the range of rifles or grenades. Yet one of the major drawbacks was its accuracy. Even with an experienced mortar crew, it generally required ten bombs to achieve a direct hit on one single target.

Wehrmacht and *Waffen SS* heavy MG 34 machine guns fitted on a sustained-fire mount overlooking an enemy position. A well sighted, well hidden and well supplied MG 34 could hold up an entire attacking regiment. This machine gun, when perfectly sighted, could inflict heavy losses on an enemy advance. Throughout the summer campaign and indeed for the rest of the war the MG 34 had tremendous stopping power against enemy infantry when deployed in the most advantageous defensive positions.

A stationary *Sd.Kfz.10* with mounted 2cm *Flak* gun has halted along a road near to the front in June or July 1943. On the folding sides of the half-track additional magazine for the gun could be carried and the single axle trailer stowing more vital equipment and magazines were normally stowed.

A group of *Sturmgeschütz* crewmen rest next to a building prior to the battle. They all wear the special field-grey uniform worn by tank destroyers and self propelled assault gun units. Note the crewman standing in the doorway wearing the new form of head-dress known as the *Einheitsfeldmutze*, which by mid 1943 was becoming universal throughout the German Army.

A column of vehicles comprising of half-tracks and light *Horch* cross-country cars have halted inside a town on the way to the front lines to prepare for the battle in early July.

Waffen SS soldiers poise prior to the opening attack along the front line. In front of the Soviet defensive fortress at Kursk stood the cream of all the German combat formations. These *SS* troops wear their familiar *SS* camouflage smocks. Throughout the Kursk offensive the professionalism and technical ability of the *SS* was second to none.

From a slit trench soldiers can be seen poised for action. The soldiers are all armed with the *Kar 98K* carbine bolt-action rifle which was the standard issue piece of weaponry supplied to the German Army throughout the war. Note the units commander surveying the terrain ahead with a pair of 6 × 4 field binoculars.

A *Pz.Kpfw.V Panther* tank onboard a special railway flat car being moved to the front. In June 1943, there were twenty-one Panzer divisions, including four *Waffen SS* divisions and two *Panzergrenadier* divisions being prepared for Operation *Zitadelle* in the Kursk salient. For this massive attack the *Panzerwaffe*, in early July, were able to muster seventeen divisions and two brigades with no less than 1,715 Panzers and 147 *Sturmegeschütz* III (*Stug*) assault guns. Each division averaged some ninety-eight Panzers and self-propelled anti-tank guns. The new *Pz.Kpfw.V 'Panther' Ausf.A* made its debut, despite production problems, which would lead to repeated breakdowns in action.

A light *Wehrmacht* machine gun crew with their MG 34 machine gun on its bipod. The primary gunner was known as the *Schütze* 1, whilst his team mate, *Schütze* 2, fed the ammunition belts and saw that the gun remained operational at all times.

A *Waffen SS* crew have utilised their 8.8cm *Flak* gun against a ground target during heavy fighting. By 1943 the deadly 8.8cm *Flak* gun was used extensively against both ground and aerial targets.

A light MG 42 machine gun crew out in a field. The train of view for the gunner must have been immense and would have certainly offered a very good opportunity for detecting enemy movement from some distance away.

The crew of a 2cm *Flak* gun scouring the sky for enemy aircraft. The gun was a very effective weapon and had a fire rate of 120–280 rounds per minute. The weapons fire rate was more than capable of dealing with not only low flying enemy aircraft, but attacking enemy troop concentrations as well.

In a dugout position somewhere on the front line is a 2cm *Flak* gun. The gun has been elevated skyward in order to protect its position against aerial attack.

On a hillside a *Waffen SS* soldier can be seen peering through a tripod mounted 6 × 30 *Sf.14Z Scherenfernrohr* (scissor binoculars). This is more than likely an artillery observation post searching for enemy targets. Each artillery battery had an observation post among the front line positions.

At a command post German officers can be seen surveying the terrain with 6 × 4 field binoculars and a rangefinder. The rangefinder was a piece of state of the art equipment for the time. It took a target's height and range plus its azimuth and angle of slant to compute its rate of change.

A photograph taken from a bunker close to the front in early July 1943. Advancing in the distance are a group of *Pz.Kpfw.IV* tanks with a full summer camouflage scheme with intact side skirts ('*Schürtzen*').

Troops pose for the camera in front of their command half-track. A half-track was mainly used to tow various ordnance from one part of the front to another. However, it was also utilised for other tasks such as towing other vehicles that had developed mechanical failure or pulling trailers full of heavy supplies, and carrying soldiers into battle.

Waffen SS troops smile for the camera after evidently catching a local pig from a nearby farm and are obviously taking it back to their unit to cook it. Eating pork and other meat was always welcome relief among the men, especially after enduring many weeks eating army rations.

Waffen SS troops sit in a field, poised to move off into action. Three of the soldiers are signalmen operating a portable radio. This device was the standard radio used at battalion and regimental level. These widely used portable radios were carried by a soldier on a specially designed back-pack frame, and, when connected to each other (upper and lower valves) via special cables, could be used on the march.

A *Waffen SS* MG 34 machine gunner positioned in a dugout in a field. The weapon has the MG 34 fifty-round basket drum magazine fitted. Although the MG 34 had been supplanted by the faster-firing MG 42, it was still considered a very effective weapon and was used extensively in Russia until the end of the war.

A soldier sleeps in front of his half-track vehicle prior to operations at Kursk in early July 1943. The vehicle has been well concealed beneath straw in order to minimise the possible threat of aerial attack.

A motorcycle combination moves along a dirt road following a column of lorries full of supplies and troops, all of which are destined for the front.

A decorated soldier poses for the camera in front of a *Marder* light tank destroyer. These vehicles served in both the *Waffen SS* and *Wehrmacht* divisional anti-tank battalions on the Eastern Front and saw some success at Kursk.

A light MG 34 machine gun crew waits on a roadside before resuming their march to the front. The term light and heavy machine guns defined the role and not the weight of the gun. Rifle squads generally had a light machine gun with a bipod, along with one or two spare barrels. A heavy machine gun group, however, had the bipod fitted machine gun, but additionally carried a tripod with optical sight.

A *Tiger* tank rolls along a road with infantry hitching a lift. The *Tiger* tank played a significant role on the Eastern Front and at Kursk the tank was distributed among the elite *Waffen SS* Panzer units where it performed very successfully. However, there were too few to make any significant gains.

The crew pose for the camera with their *Pz.Kpfw.IV*. Initially the *Panzer IV* was designed as an infantry support tank, but soon proved to be so diverse and effective that it earned a unique tactical role on the battlefield. The *Panzer IV* was an ultimate credit to the Panzer divisions it served, and was the only Panzer to stay in production throughout the war.

Waffen SS troops are seen in a dugout position in a field prior to the Kursk offensive. In Army South these elite soldiers were deployed for action, ready at a moment's notice to fight their way through the formidable lines of barbed wire entanglements, minefields and anti-tank guns.

A crew member with his stationary *Sd.Kfz.251* half-track. Despite the *Panzerwaffe*'s impressive array of firepower, there was a shortage of infantry which consequently led to Panzer units being required to take on more ambitious tasks normally preserved for the infantry.

A group of *Wehrmacht* soldiers in a dugout. One soldier can be seen armed with a stick grenade. During preparations for the offensive many thousands of these dugouts were constructed, in which the troops lived and slept for a number of days until they were finally ordered to move forward to their jump-off points.

The crew of a *Marder* III *Panzerjäger* poses for the camera. The *Marder* III was the first of a series of improvised light tank hunters, and was built on the chassis of a *Pz.Kpfw.38 (t)*. This particular vehicle is fitted with a captured 7.62cm Russian 36 anti-tank gun.

Officers scan the terrain with their 6 x 30 binoculars whilst standing inside a field in late or early July 1943. Prior to the troops moving off to their jump off assembly points it was imperative that their commanders knew the precise location of their enemy.

A specially adapted flat bed train can be seen loaded with *Tiger* tanks heading for the front line. A major factor in the success of the Panzer divisions on the Eastern Front was their ability to reach threatened sectors of the front swiftly.

An MG 34 mounted on a *Dreibein 34* anti-aircraft tripod mount can be seen in a field. A motorcycle combination and a number of *Horch* cross-country cars can be seen purposely spaced out across the field in order to reduce heavy loss to its column if there was an aerial attack.

Chapter Two

Battle Unleashed

Even as the Germans were moving their forces into place to open the attack, their enemy were already totally prepared for Operation Citadel. For three long months there had been extensive building and various preparations to counter the German attack. Improved intelligence allowed Russian commanders to predict exactly the strategic focal point of the German attack. It was this combined collection of battlefield intelligence that proved the ultimate failure of Citadel, even before the battle had been unleashed. The *Panzerwaffe* were determined to replicate their *Blitzkrieg* tactics, but the immense preparations that had gone into constructing the Soviet defences meant that the Germans were never ever going to succeed in penetrating into the strategic depths of the Red Army fortifications with any overriding success.

In addition to their defensive programme, the Red Army implemented preparations for elaborate deception plans in order to confuse the enemy. The Soviet went to great lengths to conceal their troop concentrations and defensive dispositions, which included constructing false trenches, dummy tanks and artillery, and even false airfields. All Red Army troop and rail movements were conducted at night or when visibility limited the Germans from carrying out aerial reconnaissance missions.

Traffic too in the immediate defensive area was also kept to a minimum to avoid enemy suspicion. Although these techniques did not entirely hide their extensive activities, it did cause the Germans to seriously under-estimate the strength of their enemies.

When night fell on the eve of the attack, units which were to form the first line of attack began drawing up towards the front line. Nearby the assault detachments moved up and waited with anxiety at their jumping off points. These units included sappers and infantry supported by heavy machine guns, mortars, and a number of tanks and self-propelled guns. Behind the assault detachments came advanced battalions, likewise heavily supported by tank and self-propelled gun battalions.

As the Germans completed their battle preparations, there was a general feeling, not of elation at the thought of unleashing the greatest attack thus so far on the

Eastern Front, but something more deeply ingrained, a firm belief to do their duty to the 'Fatherland' and finally turn around the deteriorating war situation.

Finally, on 5 July 1943, the pre-dawn light heralded a massive German bombardment, unleashing the battle of Kursk. The German artillery barrage was so immense that in less than an hour they had hurled more shells than they had used in the entire 1939 and 1940 Poland and Western campaigns put together. Mile after mile the front erupted in flame and smoke. The pulverising effects of the shelling caused massive death and devastation to the Red Army lines. However, in spite of this violent bombardment, Soviet artillery too soon joined the cacophony of sound and the return Russian fire soon confirmed what all the Germans feared: the attack was not a surprise. All over the front, Soviet artillery crews fired at known German artillery positions. The first troops to become embroiled in the fighting were artillery units, which fired concentration, mobile, and fixed barrage fire. As the Germans moved forward through the smoke near the forward edge, anti-tank artillery and anti-tank rifles opened-up on their advancing tanks. Mortar and machine gun fire concentrated on the enemy infantry. All of the weapons of the infantry, and the anti-tank strong points and artillery groups supporting these divisions, entered the battle to repel the enemy blows. Soviet soldiers heroically struggled with the attacking groups of enemy. The infantry skillfully destroyed tanks with grenades and bottles filled with mixtures of fuel. Under a hurricane of fire, they stole up to the German vehicles, struck them with anti-tank grenades, set them on fire with incendiary bottles, and laid mines under them. Overall, during the course of the first day, the sappers emplaced an additional 6,000 mines, which became a dreadful threat for the *Panzerwaffe*.

To the German soldier in battle, this was unlike any other engagement they had previously encountered. A German grenadier wrote: 'The Red Army soldiers refused to give up. Nor did they panic in the face of our roaring *Tiger* tanks. The Soviets were cunning in every way. They allowed our tanks to rumble past their well camouflaged foxholes and then sprang out to deal with the German grenadiers following in its wake. Constantly our tanks and assault guns had to turn back to relieve the stranded and often exhausted grenadiers'.

The initial phase of the Soviet defensive action at Kursk was often crude, messy and costly, but in a tactical and operational sense it achieved its objectives. Much of the Red Army front had held its positions against overwhelming fire power, but the attack was not over. During the rest of the day the Germans unleashed a huge attack of infantry and armoured vehicles against the Russian forward positions. All morning Russian defences endured ceaseless fire. Red Army positions were engulfed in a sea of fire and explosion as it tried to hold its front line positions. Russian troops were duty-bound to hold their lines to the death. Whilst a number of areas of the front simply cracked under the sheer weight of the German onslaught, many more Russian units demonstrated their ability to defend the most hazardous positions against well prepared and highly trained enemy forces. Red Army infantry divisions bitterly contested large areas of the countryside. Fighting was often savage resulting in heavy casualties on both sides.

Two photographs showing two different 2cm *Flakvierling* 38 positions being prepared for action. These quadruple-barreled self-propelled guns demonstrated outstanding anti-aircraft capabilities. As the war dragged on in the east many of these weapons were also be being used against ground targets, with great effect.

Three photographs showing a well placed 8.8cm *Flak* gun. This was the most famous German anti-aircraft gun of the Second World War. The gun was bolted on a cruciform platform from which it fired with outriggers extended. In one photograph the crew have utilised the weapon in a ground attack role. At Kursk the Germans had already recognised that heavier and more lethal Soviet armour had been compiled against the *Wehrmacht* and for this reason German forces had clamored to obtain more *Flak* guns that could deal with the increasing enemy threat.

Five photographs showing 8.8cm *Flak* guns during operations on the Eastern Front in the summer of 1943. With Soviet aircraft now increasing its dominance in the skies many German divisions had increased their anti-aircraft battalions, with each of them containing two or even three heavy batteries. In these photographs it shows 8.8cm *Flak* guns complete with *Schützschild* (splinter shield).

Two photographs taken the moment a *Nebeltruppe* battery launches a volley of its deadly *Nebelwerfer* rockets. Note the distinctive smoke trails the rockets temporarily leave in the air. Although designed primarily as an anti-personnel weapon, these rockets proved lethal against open and soft-skinned vehicles.

A gun crew in action with their 15cm s.IG33 artillery gun. A typical infantry regiment comprised three infantry battalions, an infantry gun company with six 7.5cm l.IG18 and two 15cm s.IG33 guns, and an anti-tank company with twelve 3.7cm Pak 35/36 guns. The 15cm s.IG33 infantry gun was regarded the workhorse pieces operated by specially trained infantrymen.

An artilleryman unloads from a vehicle 15cm shells in special wicker containers. The 15cm shell was fired from the 15cm s.FH18 heavy field howitzer. The 15cm field howitzer was primarily designed to shell targets deeper into the enemy rear. This included command posts, reserve units, assembly areas, and logistic facilities.

Three photographs showing assault pioneers flushing out an enemy defensive position. Pioneers were mainly employed as assault troops to supplement the infantry and were employed on the battlefield to attack fortifications and other defensive positions with demolitions and flamethrowers. Here a pioneer is armed with a *Flammenwerfer 35*.

Two photographs showing a *Sd.Kfz.251* half-track carrying *Waffen SS* troops to the front during the opening stages of the Kursk offensive, 'Operation Citadel' in early July 1943. In front of the Soviet defensive fortress at Kursk stood the cream of all the German combat formations.

A *Pz.Kpfw.IV* advances through a captured village during the opening operation at Kursk in the summer of 1943. For the majority of the war the *Pz.Kpfw.IV* was certainly a match for its opponent's heavy tanks, quickly and effectively demonstrating its superiority on the battlefield.

Wehrmacht troops advance forward towards strong Red Army fortifications during the opening attack. Note how the soldiers are purposely spaced apart in order to reduce the amount of casualties sustained if they were attacked either by ground or aerial bombardment.

Tanks are seen here in action in undergrowth during the first armoured contacts at Kursk. It would be during the ensuing days to come that there would be the largest tank battles fought during the Second World War.

Infantry take precautionary measures along a road and lay down beside a road whilst fighting rages ahead. These soldiers are equipped with the web battle pack carrier to which was attached their mess kit, shelter cape, and other important equipment. All of the soldiers wear the standard M1936 service uniform with the black leather infantry man's belt. Attached to the belt they wear their rifle ammunition pouches for their *Karabiner 98K* bolt action rifle.

German troops are seen passing a burning building during the initial stages of the battle. During the first day of the attack both *Wehrmacht* and their *Waffen SS* counterparts progressed well against stiff Red Army resistance. However, the first line of Russian defence seemed almost impossible to break through, in spite of strong unrelenting attacks.

An *Sd.Kfz.251* has halted and troops can be seen hastily dismounting to go into battle. By the summer of 1943, this medium half-track had become not just infantry transport to the edge of the battlefield, but also a fully-fledged fighting vehicle.

Wehrmacht troops rush forward into action against a heavily defensive position. Prior to the attack heavy artillery would have attempted to soften the enemy position in order to allow armour and then troops to move forward. However, much to the German surprise Russian resistance was often particularly very strong and this resulted in heavy casualties, both in men and equipment.

An *SS Totenkopf* (Death's Head) commander raises his arm to signal his men to move forward into action. He is armed with a captured Russian PPsH submachine gun. The initial phase of the fighting at Kursk had been very costly to the Russians, but in a tactical and operational sense it achieved its objectives. During the days that followed the Red Army began to deprive the *SS* of even tactical superiority.

An *Sd.Kfz.10* half-track is seen half submerged along a water logged road. Even during the summer periods on the Eastern Front a heavy downpour of rain could bring advancing vehicles to a crawl, which subsequently caused havoc to any German attack.

A photograph taken from a *Horch* cross-country vehicle showing an advancing motorcycle combination moving towards a Russian vehicle that has been evidently hit by anti-tank rounds, and can be seen burning. Note the squad leader armed with a submachine gun.

Waffen SS motorcyclists have halted on a road with their motorcycle combination. Motorcyclists could be found in every unit of an infantry and Panzer division, especially during the early part of the war. They were even incorporated in the divisional staffs, which included a motorcycle messenger platoon.

A *Stug.III* has halted in a field. By the summer of 1943 the *Stug.III* had become a very popular assault gun on the battlefield. The vehicles had initially provided crucial mobile fire support to the infantry, and also proved their worth as invaluable anti-tank weapons. However, by the time they were unleashed at Kursk they were primarily used as an anti-tank weapon, thus depriving the infantry of vital fire support.

Troops hug the side of a road prior to going into action. Positioned next to them are two 7.5cm *l.IG18*. This light howitzer was used in direct infantry support. The gun was very versatile in combat and the crew often aggressively positioned it, which usually meant the piece was regularly exposed on the battlefield.

A *Stug.III* in a field during the opening attack at Kursk. By this period of the war the *Stug* had been slowly absorbed into Panzer units, Panzer and *Panzergrenadier* divisions of the *Wehrmacht* and *Waffen SS*.

A nice close-up view of the *Schwerer Panzerspähwagen* (Heavy Armoured Reconnaissance vehicle). Although large it was very versatile and quick, especially on open ground. Initially the vehicle was used extensively during the early war years as the main armoured reconnaissance vehicle. However, by the summer of 1943 it was rarely seen on the battlefield.

Two photographs showing the *Leichter Panzerspähwagen* (Light Armoured Reconnaissance vehicle). This vehicle was used by reconnaissance battalions of the Panzer divisions. This vehicle was armed with the MG 34 for local defence.

In a forward observation post and a soldier can be seen looking through a pair of scissor binoculars. From this position the observer could send through details of enemy movements back to divisional headquarters.

Probably in the rear awaiting orders to prepare for action is a group of troops posing for the camera with a *Sd.Kfz.251* half-track. Note the *Pak 35/36* anti-tank gun. This weapon was the first anti-tank gun mass produced and saw service in both the *Wehrmacht* and *Waffen SS*. It was used extensively at Kursk, and went on to be used until the end of the war.

A 7.5cm *Pak 40* can be seen being towed by an *Sd.Kfz.10* half-track towards the battlefront followed by confident *Wehrmacht* troops. This deadly *Pak 40* had a spaced-armour shield held together by large bolts. These bolts had drilled holes that allowed the crews to thread foliage through them and conceal the weapon on the battlefield.

The following six photographs show various half-tracks mounting *Flak* guns. Both the single and quadruple mounted *Flak* guns were deadly pieces of weaponry. The quadruple piece for instance, which combined four guns, was served by eight men. These lethal guns were much respected by low-flying Russian airmen and were also particularly devastating against light vehicles, as well as troops caught in the open. The weapon also armed a variety of vehicles on self-propelled mounts where they could be moved from one part of the defensive line to another quickly and efficiently.

German soldiers advance cautiously. The *Stug.III* is vulnerable without infantry support; the infantry know they must keep their distance due to the fire the armour will attract.

What appears to be up-beat captured Russian prisoners being led away to the rear. Unbeknown to these soldiers their fate looked bleak. Many starved to death in hastily erected PoW camps, were transported to Poland or Germany where they were worked to death in one of the many labour camps, or agreed to join the German army.

A half-track being prepared for a march in the summer of 1943. Half-tracks were designed to primarily tow *Flak* and artillery guns, and were versatile enough to be utilised in pulling lighter ordnance, like limbers and other forms of transport mainly used by animal draught. This clearly demonstrates the *Wehrmacht*'s resourcefulness on marches.

A *Totenkopf* forward position during the initial stages of the Kursk offensive. By 7 July the advance of the *SS.Panzerkorps* seemed more promising than ever. *Totenkopf* had managed to smash through more than 30 miles of Russian line, whilst the *Leibstandarte* and *Das Reich* were equally successful despite enduring bitter fighting.

Here in this photograph a light *Waffen SS* MG 34 machine gunner can be seen concealed in undergrowth with his weapon. The machine gun has the MG 34 fifty-round basket drum magazine fitted. The term light and heavy machine guns defined the role and not the weight of the gun.

A *Sd.Kfz.230* light half-track armed with an MG 34 complete with splinter shield for local defence moves forward into action during operations in the Kursk region. The MG 34 machine gun was one of the most popular weapons used both in the *Wehrmacht* and *Waffen SS*. It had tremendous defensive stopping power against enemy infantry during the battle.

German troops in one of the many trench systems that littered the front lines at Kursk. Supporting the line is a *Pz.Kpfw.IV* with intact side skirts and a summer camouflage scheme.

A rifle squad moves forward towards a captured Russian village. A typical German infantry division consisted of three infantry regiments, an artillery regiment, reconnaissance, anti-tank, pioneer, and signal battalions, plus divisional services. Trucks transported much of the supporting battalions, but there were many infantry that marched on foot including all the supply columns that were horse-drawn.

A half-track carefully negotiates a relatively shallow river during operations in the Kursk salient. This was one of the quickest methods of crossing a river, instead of waiting for pioneers to erect a pontoon bridge.

An *Sd.Kfz.251/3 Ausf.B* complete with antennae for long range radio communication. The crew onboard more than likely belongs to a signals unit and is probably coordinating with local ground forces in the vicinity.

A *Wehrmacht* soldier armed with a M1924 stick grenade prepares to launch his weapon into action against a building that has already been set alight by either grenade, mortar or artillery fire.

Chapter Three

Northern Thrust

O n the Northern Front the German 9th Army, commanded by General Walter Model, had launched a major attack on the first day of Citadel against the Russian Central Front, which composed of the 13th Army. According to the German plan Model's 9th Army was to break through the Soviet defences, advance southwards to Kursk and link up with the northward moving 4th Panzer Army. Once the two armies had successfully joined and cut off the Soviet troops within the salient, they would then turn and destroy the enemy.

The initial phase of the 9th Army northern thrust went considerably well. Slowly and systematically, the Germans bulldozed their way through with Russian troops either fighting to the death, or saving themselves by escaping the impending slaughter by withdrawing to another makeshift position. Fighting on the Northern Front was a fierce contest of attrition, and although the Red Army had showed great fortitude and determination, they were constantly hampered by overwhelming fire power from *Tiger* and *Panther* tanks. Consequently, the remaining troops holding the lines were subjected to merciless ground and aerial bombardments. Unabated fighting continued and losses were massive. Slowly and systematically the Red Army lines were pulverised. Those troops fortunate enough to escape the impending slaughter immediately found themselves in open hostile countryside with lurking Panzers inflicting terrible casualties on them.

By the end of the first day of the battle, the Germans had broken through the first line of Soviet defences and created a gap almost 10 miles wide and 5 miles deep. Fighting however, intensified as the Germans exploited the receding front lines by methodically reducing the Russian defences to a bombed and blasted rubble. The ferocity of the German attacks were immense and without respite. After twenty-four hours of almost continuous battle the Russian soldier was exhausted and fighting for survival in a number of places. Russian commanders had insisted that their troops were to fight from fixed position without any tactical retreat, but as a consequence this had caused some units to become encircled by German rifle divisions, leaving tank units to speed past unhindered and achieve deeper penetrations.

By the next day the Germans had made considerable progress in a number of areas and had battered the Red Army forward defensive positions. In fact, the fighting had been so severe that the *Panzerkorps* had pushed the Russians back some 4 miles along a front of more than 8 miles. In these areas of the front the Red Army were experiencing defensive problems, and in spite of strong fortified positions, which were manned with anti-tank guns and lines of machine gun pits, the Germans moved forward in their hundreds regardless of the cost in life. It soon became apparent to the Russian commanders that afternoon that their enemy might succeed in overrunning their defensive lines and spilling out into the salient and cutting off a number of troop concentrations. In some units there were no more reserves or reinforcements to help bolster the struggling defensive lines.

Over the next couple of days the situation for the Red Army still looked grim. All along the battered and blasted front the Soviet troops continued to try in vain to hold their positions. For the German commanders the campaign had progressed well and their men continued to exploit the Russian defences. Between Ponyri and Soborovka, for instance, the main German tank force boasted some 1,000, tanks, 3,000 guns and mortars and 5,000 machine guns. However, they were confronted by an even greater enemy force. The Russians were determined to hold at all costs and repel the attackers using a variety of heavy and light artillery pieces supported by assault guns and groups armed with anti-tank mines and other weapons to halt the advancing panzers.

The German northern thrust had been a fierce contest of attrition, and although the Germans had showed great fortitude and determination, they were constantly hampered by the lack of weapons and manpower needed to sustain them on the battlefield against an overwhelming enemy force and massive array of fortifications. Over the next few days Model's 9th Army tried to seize the initiative by taking the town of Ponyri in a large tank battle. But the Red Army were well armed and well dug-in and because they had laid an extensive minefield the Panzers failed to accomplish any of its objects.

By 10 July Model's 9th Army had little chance of reaching Kursk. After five long days of almost continuous battle the German soldier was exhausted and in some areas fighting for survival. By this period of the battle Model's military situation had become increasingly desperate. Whilst many areas of the front had simply cracked under the sheer weight of the German onslaught, there had been many more Russian units that had been able to demonstrate their ability to defend the most hazardous positions against some of the fiercest tank assaults of the entire campaign. Russian infantry divisions had bitterly contested large areas of the countryside. Fighting was often savage resulting in terrible casualties on both sides. The 9th Army was significantly damaged with high losses, and as a result Model was forced to maintain the defensive until the situation was rectified. He hoped that in the south the southern thrust would draw off heavy pressure in the north and allow his forces to renew their offensive actions once more and take Kursk.

Two photographs showing probably the most famous German tank associated with the Kursk offensive, a Mark VI 'Tiger'. The Tiger tank was probably the most famous Panzer in the Panzerwaffe and was nicknamed by the troops as the 'furniture van' because of its sheer size. During the last two years of the war the Panzerwaffe would extensively use the Tiger in a number of prominent roles in both major offensive and defensive employments.

The *Pz.Kpfw.IV* played a prominent role during the Kursk offensive. Despite inferior numbers, the tank performed well in various operations and achieved resounding success, especially within the ranks of the elite *Waffen SS* divisions.

The crew of the new Mark V 'Panther' tank pose for the camera in 1943. The *Panther* first made its debut on the Eastern Front at Kursk in July 1943. The *Panther* was rushed into battle before it was fully ready for combat.

During a lull in the fighting and the crew of an *Sd.Kfz.251* half-track have time to relax. One of the rear doors of the vehicle is open, and the tarpaulin that protects the crew compartment can be seen rolled back.

A *Hummel* during operations at Kursk. The vehicle displays a summer camouflage scheme. The *Hummel* mounted a standard 15cm heavy field howitzer in a lightly armoured fighting compartment built on *Pz.Kpfw.III/IV* composite chassis. This heavy self-propelled gun carried only eighteen 15cm rounds, but was a potent weapon against Soviet armour.

The crew of a 15cm s.FH18 howitzer is seen in action. Normally before any armoured strike or infantry attack, artillery crews concentrated on enemy concentration areas, unleashing their fire-power where anti-tank units were suspected to be located. Each *Abteilung* comprised of three firing batteries with each battery containing four howitzers.

A heavy MG42 machine gun position. The battle of the Kursk was probably the first modern Soviet operation of the war. Despite the fact that the Red Army lacked the technological superiority of individual weapons, they had a well-prepared defensive programme, which included elaborate deception plans to confuse the enemy.

A battery of 15cm heavy field howitzers in a field. The artillery bombardment that opened up the German offensive at Kursk was massive. After it subsided infantry and armour poured forward with artillery units following in the wake of the forward spearheads.

Germans load a 5cm *Pak 38* anti-tank gun, seriously outdated by the time of Kursk.

An MG 34 machine gunner positioned in a field with bipod lying next to his number two. Although the MG 34 had been supplanted by the faster-firing MG 42, it was still considered a very effective weapon and was used extensively in Russia until the end of the war.

An *Sd.Kfz.251* half-track hurtles across a field passing a burning building. The half-track was probably the most common armoured vehicle in the German arsenal, and during the Kursk offensive it played a prominent role in both towing ordnance and transporting troops.

A late variant *Pz.Kpfw.III* moves along a road during operations in the early summer of 1943. During the initial stages of the invasion of Russia the *Pz.Kpfw.III* showed its worth. However, against formidable Russian armour such as the T-34 medium and the KV-1 heavy tanks, the *Pz.Kpfw.III* was soon recognised as an inadequate weapon in the ranks of the *Panzerwaffe*.

A *Tiger* tank advances along a road. The *Tiger* entered service in August 1942 and soon gained a superb fighting record. The mighty *Tiger* played a key role in the German offensive at Kursk.

A *Sturmgeschütz* troop in a gully somewhere in the Kursk region in early July. From 1943 until the end of the war the assault guns were slowly absorbed into the Panzer units, Panzer and *Panzergrenadier* divisions of the *Wehrmacht* and *Waffen SS*.

A *Pz.Kpfw.IV* has parked next to the side of a dirt track hugging a line of trees to help conceal it from aerial detection. The tank appears to have seen considerable action as it only retains one section of its side skirt armour.

Two *Stug.III tanks are seen advancing into action during an enemy contact. Because the Stug.III* had been in constant demand in Russia, Hitler ordered that the assault gun be up-gunned and up-armoured with a longer more potent 7.5cm gun. This more powerful assault gun went into production in mid-1942. The *Ausf.F* variant mounted a 7.5cm *Stuk 40 L/43* gun. The following year the final *Stug* variant, the *Ausf.G,* entered the *Panzerwaffe* and was rushed into service. Many of the *Stugs* to see service at Kursk were the *Ausf.G* variant.

A command half-track with long range radio antenna moves forward into action. For local defence the vehicle is armed with a MG 34 machine gun with splinter shield.

A variety of half-tracks advance along a road toward the battlefront. The half-track had become not just a vehicle to tow ordnance and transport infantry to the edge of the battlefield, but also performed as a self-propelled gun.

Troops rest next to an *Sd.Kfz.10* half-track armed with a mounted 2cm *Flak* gun. Anti-aircraft defences came into prominence from late 1941, as Soviet Air Force started to inflict heavy casualties. By the time the Kursk offensive began both the *Wehrmacht* and *Waffen SS* mechanised formations had become well equipped with *Flak* guns.

The mortar crew of an 8.14cm GrW 34 pose for the camera in a dug out position. Each battalion fielded six of these excellent mortars, which could fire fifteen bombs per minute to a range of 2,625 yards.

A *Waffen SS Stug.III Ausf.G* tows a vehicle up a steep gradient. In spite of the numerous advantages of the assault guns, equipping the Panzer units with these vehicles did not blend well with the nature of the Panzer. Yet, because of the lack of tanks in the dwindling ranks of the Panzer divisions, the *Stug.III* was used alongside the turreted tanks until the end of the war.

Panzergrenadiere in action. The *Sd.Kfz.251* medium half-track could carry a full rifle squad as well as its crew of two. But lightly armoured and open-topped, it was vulnerable on the battlefield. On reaching the forward edge of the battlefield, the grenadiers would quickly dismount and disperse while the vehicle provided covering fire.

A Panzer crewman wearing the familiar black Panzer field cap questions a captured Russian tank man and crew. At Kursk the Red Army had massed some 3,600 tanks and although losses were huge there, arsenal and extensive defensive positions were enough to stem the German onslaught.

Well concealed in a field is a quadruple-barrelled self-propelled anti-aircraft gun. By the summer of 1943, mechanised formations were well equipped with *Flak* guns. There were motorised *Flak* battalions, with divisions being furnished with additional anti-aircraft platoons and companies in the *Panzergrenadier*, Panzer and artillery regiments. This *Flak* gun was a formidable weapon and was more than capable of combating both low flying aircraft and ground targets.

Here a *Nashorn* ('rhinoceros') 8.8cm heavy *Panzerjäger* photographed in action against an enemy target. The high profile of the *Nashorn* made it hard to conceal, but its long-range gun enabled it to engage at a longer ranges than other tank destroyers. Between early 1943 and March 1945, only 474 *Nashorn* were produced.

A *Wespe* self-propelled artillery piece climbs a steep gradient as it goes into action. This versatile vehicle was armed with a 10.5cm *leFH 18/2 L/28* gun and protected by a lightly armoured superstructure mounted on a chassis of a *Pz.Kpfw.II*. This vehicle served in armoured artillery battalions but were lightly armoured, and as a result many of them were lost in battle.

An interesting photograph showing a large column of armoured vehicles advancing across a field. Visible are the *Sd.Kfz.251* half-track, *Pz.Kpfw.II*, and *Sd.Kfz.10* mounting a *Flak* gun.

Two *Sturmgeschütz* advance across a field. Although the *Stug* proved excellent against any Soviet tank at long to medium range, they were vulnerable to attacks from Soviet infantry since they lacked any internal machine gun for close defence.

A *Panzergrenadier* aids an injured comrade from an *Sd.Kfz.251* half-track. German infantry had found the advance into enemy lines very difficult in a number of places. Due to extensive well armed defensive positions the Germans incurred huge casualties and as a result were sometimes forced to withdraw.

An *Sd.Kfz.251* advances past a destroyed Russian position. In spite of the huge losses in Russian artillery the Red Army arsenal was large enough to cope with the significant losses. Throughout the battle of Kursk the Red Army was determined to grind down attacking German units with a combination of mines and artillery fire whatever the cost. Indirect fire from howitzers would stop the German infantry, while direct fire from massed 45mm, 57mm, and 85mm anti-tank guns and 76.2mm divisional field guns could often stop the tanks.

An *Sd.Kfz.251* half-track armed with a mounted 2.8cm anti-tank gun moves forward into action, passing a mortar crew who are preparing their 8.14cm mortar for action. The mortar's intended role was to engage pockets of resistance that were beyond the range of hand grenades. It was designed for high angled fire only. The main drawbacks of the weapon were its inadequate range and the limited effectiveness of its ammunition, which was regarded as not heavy enough.

Halted *Sd.Kfz.251* half-tracks are purposely spaced out across the Russian steepe in order to minimise the threat of aerial attack.

Three photographs showing an *Sd.Kfz.10/4* moving forward into action. Mounted on the back of the half-track is a 2cm *Flak* gun. In two of the photographs the vehicle is towing an *Sd.Ah.51* ammunition trailer.

A *Pz.Kpfw.IV* has halted on a road somewhere in the Kursk salient during operations in early July. Because the German armour in the north was heavily concentrated and used with much more intensity than in the south, German armour losses were much heavier.

A half-track can be seen towing a 15cm heavy field howitzer. As the standard heavy field howitzer in the *Wehrmacht*, the gun was very effective at clearing up heavily concentrated positions to let tanks and infantry pour through unhindered.

A *Pz.Kpfw.IV* can be seen halted at the side of a road with other stationary vehicles from an unidentified unit. The German armoured attack in the north had nearly broken through the main Soviet defence zones, but stalled due to heavy Russian resistance. The Soviet counter-offensive soon forced Model to withdraw or risk the destruction of both German armies.

An *Sd.Kfz.251* half-track mounting a short-barrelled 7.5cm gun has halted on the vast Russian steepe. One of the crewmembers is cleaning the gun barrel. Note the crude yellow camouflage spots painted over the vehicle in order to try and blend the half-track with the local summer vegetation.

A photograph taken from a *Stug.III* showing the mighty 7.5cm long barrelled gun. In the distance other *Stug.III* tanks can be seen moving across the terrain.

Moving towards the battlefront is an artillery truppen armed with a 10.5cm *le.FH16* light field howitzer, which is being towed by a half-track. The wheels on the artillery piece consisted of a heavy duty cast steel with a solid rubber rim. This type of design allowed the gun to be towed at relatively high-speed by a motorised vehicle.

A *Junker 52* (Ju-52) transport aircraft departs from a temporary landing strip. Whilst the Ju-52 replenished much needed supplies and troops to the front and airlifted wounded personnel, the aircraft was slow and very lightly armed against fighters. As a result, it suffered terrible losses in almost all actions on the Eastern Front. Many types of replacement were built, but none was as popular or reliable as the Ju-52.

Chapter Four

Southern Thrust

In the south the German attack through the Kursk salient progressed considerably better than in the north. It was here in the south that the *Wehrmacht* and *Panzerwaffe* were supported by the elite formations of the *Waffen SS*. In front of the Soviet defensive fortress stood the cream of all the German combat formations at Kursk, the premier divisions of the *Waffen SS*. Here, the *2.SS.Panzerkorps*, commanded by *SS-Obergruppenführer* Paul Hausser, formed part of the 4th Panzer Army. The corps comprised of the three premiere *Waffen SS* divisions, *1.SS.Leibstandarte Adolf Hitler*, *2.SS.Das Reich* and the *3.SS.Totenkopf*. The three divisions had a line strength of 390 of the latest tanks and 104 assault guns between them, including forty-two of the Army Group's *Tigers* tanks. At their starting positions, the three *SS* divisions covered a sector that was 12 miles wide. The *Totenkopf* occupied the left flank of the advance, the *Leibstandarte* was in the centre and *Das Reich* held the right.

Within hours of the artillery bombardment, the three *Waffen SS* divisions were engaged in the opening stages of the greatest armoured clash in history. The task of the *SS.Panzerkorps* was to advance via Beresov and Sadeynoye, and break through the first defensive belt. Between Lutchki and Jakovlevo was the second line of Russian defensive positions, and when these were destroyed the advance would follow in a general northeastern direction. For this operation the 167nd Infantry Division would form part of the *SS* corps and would guard the left flank. The *Leibstandarte*'s first attack went well, and their armour soon encircled enemy units that were destroyed with supporting grenadiers. The 9th Company of the *Leibstandarte*'s *2.SS.Panzergrenadier* Regiment captured two hills west of Byelgorod and took five fortified positions with explosive charges. The soldiers of the *Totenkopf* division too wasted no time and smashed onto a series of strong Soviet defence lines. At the same time the *Das Reich* division made considerable progress, and infiltrated enemy lines in front of them.

By evening of the first day of the attack *Totenkopf*, with its new *Tiger* tanks leading the advance, had reached the second Russian defensive belt and managed to capture the village of Yakhontovo and had taken an important command post of the Soviet 69th Army. Both the *Leibstandarte* and *Das Reich* had done equally as well. With their *Tiger* and *Panzer.IV* tanks they had penetrated some 13 miles into the Russian defences. By 7 July, the advance of the *SS.Panzer Corps seemed more promising than ever. Totenkopf* had managed to smash its way through more than 30 miles of Russian line, whilst the *Leibstandarte* and *Das Reich* were equally successful despite enduring bitter fighting. *SS* battle reports confirmed that given the amount of Soviet prisoners taken and the damage inflicted on their lines, it appeared that the *SS.Panzerkorps* was poised on the edge of victory. However, they had not even yet encountered the main enemy positions. The fact that they had advanced at such speed had enabled the Russians to take full advantage of attacking the *SS* flanks.

Elsewhere on the frontline the *Wehrmacht* and especially the *Panzerwaffe* caused considerable destruction against the first lines of Russian defence. As a direct result of the German ferocity, condition of the Red Army troops varied considerably. Whilst some areas of the front were demoralised often without sufficient weapons, other parts were heavily defended with a formidable force. For days dotted along the front were a motley assorted collection of Soviet soldiers engaged in a bitter blood-thirsty battle, trying in varying degrees of bravery to repulse the never ending stream of German troops and armour. Soldiers that had been embroiled in heavy contact with the enemy for long periods often found that their rear positions had already been evacuated. As a result the troops were regularly exposed to heavier fire without support, and in many circumstances were quickly encircled and then destroyed. *Tiger* and *Panther* tanks supported by well armed grenadiers continued with unabated ferocity to smash the Russian defences. It seemed that the battle of Kursk would soon be won. However, the Germans had totally underestimated the strength and depth of the Russian defences. Within days the Russians had managed to ground down many of the *Wehrmacht* units, including those in the *SS.Panzerkorps*, and throw its offensive timetable completely off schedule. It was here on the blood-soaked plains at Kursk that for the first time in the war the Red Army had savagely contested every foot of ground and was finally on an equal footing. Through sheer weight of Soviet strength and stubborn combat along an ever-extending front, the German mobile units were finally being forced to a standstill.

On 9 July, the *SS.Panzerkorps* renewed their offensive against very strong enemy forces. In the vicious battle that ensued, the *SS* received a series of sustained attacks, but fanatically held their ground. Although they were in danger of being cut-off and encircled, they received orders to push forward and attack Soviet troops northeast of Beregovoy. During the advance, *Das Reich* guarded the eastern flank of *Totenkopf* and *Leibstandarte*. En route it became embroiled in thick bitter fighting in a huge tank battle in the hills around Prokhorovka on 12 July. Here the Soviet 5th Guard and 5th Guard Tank Armies clashed with the powerful armoured *SS* units, consequently resulting in the climax of Operation 'Zitadelle'. Throughout the attack the profes-sionalism and technical ability of the *SS* was second to none. During the heavy fighting

SS troops were often able to turn the balance even when the Russians had overwhelming superiority in numbers. In spite of the losses the units were imbued with optimism and continued to deliver to the enemy heavy blows.

During the climax of the battle both the *Totenkopf* and *Leibstandarte* attacked, whilst *Das Reich* remained on the defensive, repelling a number of armour and infantry attacks. Although Russian losses in both men and equipment far exceeded the German, their losses could be replaced. German losses, however, except where armour could be recovered, were total. Within less than a week of *Zitadelle* being unleashed both sides had lost several hundred tanks and thousands of troops. While the Red Army was able to repair and replace its losses, the SS divisions had to struggle on with what they had left at their disposal. Constantly, the soldiers were being slowly ground down in a battle of attrition. The Russians had committed no less than seven corps, with more than 850 tanks and SU-85 assault guns. Wave upon wave of Russian T-34 tanks poured a storm of fire onto the SS positions. When the Soviet tanks run out of ammunition, the crews often physically rammed the German tanks. Dismounted tanks crews then set about destroying the Panzers on foot using all weapons at their disposal, including grenades and mines.

Similar battles of attrition were fought in many parts of the *2.SS.Panzerkorps*, but it was the soldiers of the *Leibstandarte* that were taking the brunt of the fighting. Everywhere enemy troops charged the SS positions, turning these once mighty soldiers from attackers to desperate defenders. The division's *1.SS.Panzergrenadier Regiment* had no sooner attacked and captured an important position, when it was repeatedly struck by waves of Russian tanks and mounted infantry and compelled to go over to the defensive.

By 13 July, the *2.SS.Panzerkorps* was unable to make any further progress, and poor ground conditions were hampering its re-supply efforts. As a consequence Russian forces managed to drive back the *3.Panzerdivision* in the area of the Rakovo-Kruglik road and recaptured hill 247, and the town of Berezovka. The following day, *Totenkopf* was forced out of its bridgehead on the northern bank of the Psel River, while further east *Das Reich* had made limited progress, capturing the town of Belenichino. The *Grossdeutschland* Division was ordered to attack westwards, in order to recapture the ground lost by the *3.Panzerdivision*. Following another day of bitter fighting the division finally managed to link up with *3.Panzerdivision* at Berezovka, but it was unable to dislodge Russian forces from Hill 247.

On 15 July, *Das Reich* made contact with the *7.Panzerdivision*. However, the Russian offensive to the north of the salient was now threatening the 9th Army rear and it was forced to begin a planned withdrawal westwards to avoid encirclement. Following its withdrawal, almost all offensive action around Prokhorovka ceased and German forces in the area went over to the defensive. The battle of Kursk now seemed irretrievably lost.

A vehicle towing part of a pontoon section moves along a road which has seen some considerable action. In order for the Germans to sustain their momentum on the battlefield it was often paramount that pioneers kept pace with the advance echelons of an armoured drive in order to rapidly construct pontoons across rivers, and allow vital traffic to cross unhindered.

An *Sd.Kfz.251* half-track advances along a road passing through a village. The crew have applied bundles of corn on the fenders of the vehicle and parts of the engine cover in order to try and break up the distinctive shape and help conceal it from aerial reconnaissance.

Two photographs taken in sequence showing *Waffen SS* troops and armoured vehicles mainly comprising of *Sd.Kfz.251* half-tracks. All of the vehicles are purposely spaced out across the battlefield in order to reduce the threat of an aerial attack.

An *Sd.Kfz.6/2* half-track armed with a
3.7cm *Flak 36/37* has halted somewhere
near the front line. The vehicle normally
towed a special trailer, *Sd.Ah.57*, which
carried the bulk of the *Flak* gun's
ammunition.

Two *Waffen SS* soldiers escort a
captured Russian prisoner to the rear,
probably for interrogation purposes.
The leading *SS* soldier, who is a squad
leader, is armed with an MP38 or 40
submachine gun, whilst the soldier
behind him is armed with an MG 34
machine gun.

An interesting photograph showing a number of VW Type 166 *Schwimmwagen*. These amphibious four-wheel drive off-roaders were used extensively by both the *Wehrmacht* and the *Waffen SS* throughout the war. The Type 166 was the most numerous mass-produced amphibious car to roll off the assembly plants in Germany.

In a forward observation post somewhere on the front line and a *Waffen SS* soldier can be seen looking through a pair of 6 × 30 field binoculars.

A group of *Waffen SS* motorcyclists, probably from the famous *Totenkopf* Division, is seen standing next to one of their motorcycles. Three of the soldiers wear the motorcycle waterproof coat which was a double-breasted rubberised item of clothing. It was made of cotton twill coated rubber, with watertight seams and the coat was worn over the service uniform. The coat was loose fitting and the ends of the garment could be easily gathered in around the wearer's legs and buttoned into position, which allowed easier and safer movement whilst riding the motorcycle. The motorcycle coat was grey-green in colour and had a woolen field-grey material collar with large pockets. When in use the wearer normally wore the army canvas and leather issue gloves or mittens. Normal leather army boots were often worn.

A group of troops pose for the camera next to a heavily camouflaged VW Type.82 *Kfz.1* on 11 July 1943, near Prokhorovka. The soldiers belong to *2.SS-Panzer Division Das Reich*, and it would be here at Prokhorovka that one of the greatest tank battles in history would be unleashed on 12 July.

A *Waffen SS Sd.Kfz.251* half-track armed with a 7.5cm short gun barrel of a *Pz.Kpfw.IV* during operations at Kursk in July 1943. Note the white painted kill rings on the barrel of the 7.5cm gun.

Waffen SS troops with a flamethrower have captured a Russian position during intensive fighting. In spite of a number of successful engagements by the Waffen SS, the Red Army remained very strong and was clearly demonstrating that they were rapidly developing into a skilful army with enormous quantities of men and material.

An MG 34 heavy machine gun on a tripod for long range firing covers an advancing rifle company. The infantry battalion's machine gun company had two heavy machine gun platoons, each with four guns. In open terrain they would protect the flanks of advancing rifle companies, as in this photograph.

A soldier inside a dug-out prepares to fire one of the projectiles against an enemy target. It was very common for infantry, especially during intensive long periods of action, to fire their mortar from either trenches or dug-in positions where the mortar crew could also be protected from enemy fire.

An SS artillery crew prepares to fire a projectile from their 7.5cm *le.IG 18* artillery gun. This weapon could not only be fired quickly and accurately but also had an advantage on the battlefield by having a low profile design and splinter shield.

A *Waffen SS* MG 42 machine gunner and his team in a trench overlooking an enemy position. When times and conditions allowed, machine gun crews invariably prepared a number of positions. They appreciated the full value of the MG 42, and along these positions the machine gunners were able to set-up advantageous offensive and defensive positions.

A group of *Waffen SS* troops in a trench along a typical German position at Kursk in the summer of 1943. On a clear day troops were able to identify enemy positions across miles of flat terrain often without the aid of field binoculars. This was regularly to the advantage of the defender, and as a result of the terrain factor many losses were incurred by German troops moving into action.

Waffen SS troops, one of them riding on a motorcycle, have captured a group of Russian soldiers during the last phase of the Kursk offensive.

Here *Waffen SS* troops move forward into action in the Kursk salient. This would be the last major offensive operation undertaken by the Germans in the East. What would follow in its wake would be almost two years of bitter, bloody defensive battles with the *Waffen SS* being rushed to one disintegrating sector of the front to another, plugging the gaps and fighting to the death in order to slow down the inevitable advance of the Red Army.

A *Waffen SS* soldier armed with a captured Soviet PPSh submachine gun. In the field, the PPSh was a durable, low-maintenance weapon that could fire 900 rounds/min. Some 6,000,000 of these weapons were produced by the end of the war, and the Soviets would often equip whole regiments and even entire divisions with the weapon, giving them unmatched short-range firepower. The gun had proven such an effective weapon on the battlefield that both the *Wehrmacht* and *Waffen SS* used captured stocks extensively throughout fighting on the Eastern Front.

A photograph taken the moment a 15cm s.IG33 gun opens fire against an enemy target during bitter fighting in the southern sector of the Kursk salient. This particular infantry gun was a reliable and robust weapon and was used extensively by the *Waffen SS* until the end of the war.

A *Waffen SS* mortar crew are about to fire a light 5cm GrW 36 mortar against a Soviet target.

An MG 42 machine gunner, carrying a spare barrel which can be seen slung over his back, is positioned in a trench somewhere on the front line. Through sheer weight of Soviet strength and stubborn combat along an ever-extending front, the German mobile units were finally being forced to a standstill. As a result, both *SS* and *Wehrmacht* troops used trenches to mount various attacks.

A *Waffen SS* machine gun crew with their MG 34 machine gun. The primary gunner was known as the *Schütze* 1, whilst his team mate, *Schütze* 2, fed the ammunition belts and saw that the gun remained operational at all times.

A *Waffen SS* squad leader, or *Rottenführer*, confers with his men prior to going into action. Throughout the Kursk offensive the professionalism and technical ability of the *SS* was second to none.

Pz.Kpfw.IV advance across a field towards the battlefront. The *Panzerwaffe*'s failure at Kursk resulted in huge losses of tanks and material. After the battle only five *Wehrmacht* Panzer divisions and one *Waffen SS* Panzer division were sent as replacements to the Eastern Front in the latter half of 1943.

A *Waffen SS* motorcyclist smiles for the camera wearing his distinctive *Waffen SS* summer camouflage tunic and M1935 helmet cover. He is equipped with aviator goggles, 6 × 30 field binoculars and is armed with the standard infantryman's weapon, the *Kar 98K* bolt action rifle.

Grenadiers accompany an armoured personnel carrier towards the battlefront. By the 8th July German commanders in the field began to seriously doubt the success of the Kursk offensive. Prior to the attack they had not totally realised just how strong their opponent's defences were, and just how many men and weaponry the Soviets had at their disposal.

Waffen SS troops can be seen operating in a field along with two *Stug.III Ausf.G* assault guns. With the help of dive-bombers and anti-tank cannons, the SS divisions at Kursk were able to penetrate more deeply than other formations, in the process repelling a series of armoured attacks.

A *Hummel* advances into action. Some 100 *Hummel* participated in the Kursk offensive and were successful in a number of fierce engagements. They served in armoured artillery battalions or *Panzerartillerie Abteilungen* of the Panzer divisions, forming separate heavy self-propelled artillery batteries, each with six *Hummel* and one ammunition carrier.

Wehrmacht troops march into action supported by a number of armoured vehicles. By the second week of the battle, fighting in many areas was slow and very costly in both men and material. Many foot soldiers soon became entangled in strong enemy defences and loss in men was horrendous.

A number of armoured personnel carriers and other vehicles have halted in a field during a lull in the fighting. One Sd.Kfz.250 light half-track can be seen with one of the crewmen asleep on the front of the vehicle. Note the national flag draped over the rear for aerial recognition.

A half-track advances at speed past a burning building. The vehicle is towing an anti-tank gun, the 5cm *Pak 38*. A motorcyclist and other vehicles can be seen in the column.

Waffen SS Panzergrenadiere move past destroyed Soviet T-34 tanks. The Red Army fielded some 2,000,000 men and over 5,000 tanks, an extremely potent array of military hardware. The Soviets were completely prepared for the German offensive, thanks to intelligence provided by an extremely effective spy network.

Numerous *Pz.Kpfw.IV* advance forward into action during the latter stages of Kursk. All the tanks still retain their side skirts, or *Schürtzen*, which was primarily designed to prevent anti-tank shells penetrating the wheels and tracks and disabling the vehicle.

Wehrmacht troops march along a dusty road bound for the front lines. The amount of dust clouds caused by heavy troop and armoured movement often located their position, and as a direct result artillery gunners and aircraft were able to attack with more accuracy.

A *Tiger* tank has halted next to a building, probably to afford some kind of concealment whilst its crew prepares their vehicle for another push forward against heavy Russian defences. Note the tank's smoke candle dischargers attached to the side of the turret.

A *Stug.III.Ausf.G* assault gun advances across a field at speed. It has an interesting summer camouflage scheme of dark yellow base with bands of olive green. From 1943 until the end of the war the assault guns were slowly absorbed into the Panzer units, Panzer and Panzer grenadier divisions of the *Wehrmacht* and *Waffen SS*.

A *Tiger* tank belonging to the premier *Waffen SS Das Reich* Panzer Division rolls forward into action with *SS* troops on foot. *SS* Panzer and *Panzergrenadier* divisions had become known as the 'fire brigade' of the Third Reich. Wherever they were committed to battle, they attacked. Sometimes the outcome was successful, but there were many times when they failed.

A *Stug.III.Ausf.G* attached to a *Waffen SS* unit. The assault gun has a summer camouflage scheme of dark yellow base with bands of olive green. Note half of the armoured skirting is missing, these light panels were easily ripped off.

By the latter stages of Kursk, the military situation was becoming more calamitous and it was fast becoming clear how rapidly the German armoured force was diminishing. The Russian defensive positions had become so difficult to penetrate that forward *Sturmgeschütz* units became increasingly confused and entangled in bitter bloody fighting. Here in this photo a *Stug.III* has halted in a field and a captured Red Army soldier moves forward into captivity.

An interesting photograph showing *Sd.Kfz.251* in action. Note the *Ausf.B* half-track armed with the 3.7cm *Pak 35/36* anti-tank gun. By this period of the war more German half-tracks were mounting various weaponry in order to deal with the growing might of the Red Army.

Two photographs taken in sequence showing *Pz.Kpfw.IV* moving along a dirt track towards the battlefront. In order to break up the distinctive shape of the tank, the crew has applied foliage over parts of the vehicle.

Somewhere in the Kursk salient two stationary late *Pz.Kpfw.III* can be seen in a field. One of the tanks is a command vehicle and has been fitted out with long range radio antennae. Commanding officers can be seen conversing, one holding a map board.

A *Pz.Kpfw.IV Ausf.G* halted on the Russian Steppe. The vehicle carries the old 1940 divisional emblem for the 4th Panzer Division painted in yellow on the side of the turret. The emblem is a standing bear. During the battle of Kursk the *4.Panzerdivision* lost nearly 40 percent of it Panzer force.

Panzergrenadiere have hitched a lift on board a *Pz.Kpfw.IV*. The vehicle's side skirts are still intact. These skirts were constructed of mild steel plates and were very effective against close range enemy anti-tank rifles and hollow-charge explosive shells.

During a temporary lull in the fighting, the crew of a *Pz.Kpfw.III* make minor repairs to their vehicle. During the battle of Kursk seven Panzer divisions in total were annihilated, with terrible effect on the German war effort.

A *Pz.Kpfw.III* command tank has halted on the Steppe with other armoured vehicles during the latter period of the battle.

A *Pz.Kpfw.III* command tank wades across a river towards the battlefront. In relatively shallow water the Panzer was a very versatile machine. However, quite often the engine was prone to water flooding, causing a number of mechanical and electrical failures.

Pz.Kpfw.IV move forward during the latter period of the battle. Note the Pz.Kpfw.IV with side skirt armour also carrying a line of steel M1935 helmets on the back of the engine deck for additional armoured protection.

A half-track negotiates a steep gradient. The vehicle is armed with a 2cm *Flak* gun. Note one of the crewmembers trying to hold the ammunition boxes in an attempt to prevent them from sliding off the vehicle. The hinged sides are down along with the rear railings, which indicates that this vehicle is ready for action.

A *Nashorn* tank destroyer hiding in some foliage during its debut at Kursk. The *Nashorn*'s gun was one of the most effective anti-tank guns deployed during the war. Its tungsten carbide-cored sub-calibre round, *PzGr.40/43*, was capable of penetrating 190mm of rolled steel armour at a 30-degree angle of impact at a distance of 1,000 metres. The gun's tremendous performance enabled *Nashorn* to engage enemy tanks while they still were out of range themselves. These potent vehicles were issued to the schwere *Panzerjäger-Abteilungen* (specialised anti-tank battalions).

Wehrmacht troops examine the destruction wrought on horse drawn transport during the latter phase of the battle. In spite of the impressive amount of German armour at Kursk, there was a considerable amount of animal draught pressed into service and used as support.

A *Stug.III* advances across the vast Russian Steppe towards an enemy position. By the time the *Stug.III* saw action at Kursk, it had become a very common assault gun on the battlefield. It was at Kursk that it showed its true capabilities as a tank killer.

A *Tiger* tank advances through a destroyed Russian town. The heavy armoured plating of the *Tiger* was more resistant to combat damage than other lighter tanks and with a well equipped maintenance company they could be returned to the battlefield swiftly.

A half-track negotiates a gradient on the way to the front lines. The vehicle is towing a 10.5cm howitzer, one of the most common artillery pieces used in the *Wehrmacht*'s arsenal during the war.

A *Waffen SS* position overlooking ground littered with destroyed Russian and German equipment. These soldiers probably belong to the *Das Reich* division. They wear the 'Plane Tree' pattern camouflage helmet cover and a 'Palm' pattern camouflage smock.

A number of vehicles are purposely spread out across the Russian steppe in order to present a smaller target in case of bombing by ground or aerial attack.

One of two photographs taken in sequence showing an SS soldier standing over a Russian soldier who can be seen tending to his wounded comrade. Behind them a T-34/76 Model 1943 can be seen in flames.

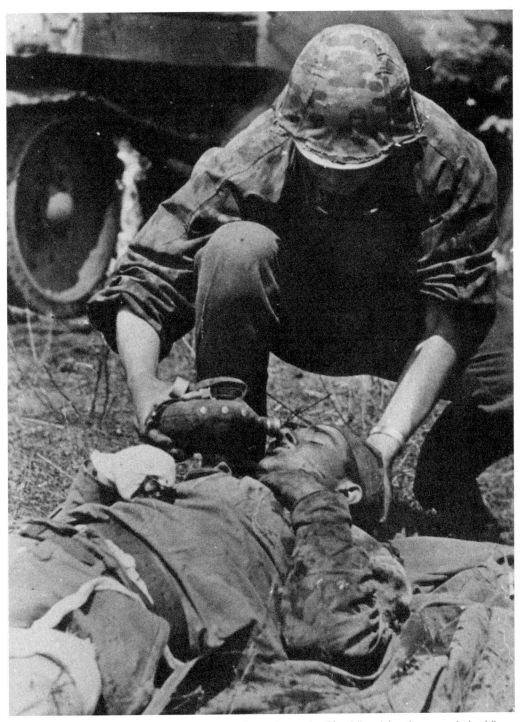

The second photograph, taken a few moments later, shows the SS soldier giving the wounded soldier a drink from his field flask. It is quite probable that these photographs was staged for the camera.

Aftermath

The reverberations caused by the defeat at Kursk meant that German forces in the south bore the brunt of the heaviest Soviet drive. Both the Russian Voronezh and Steppe Fronts possessed massive local superiority against everything the Germans had on the battlefield, and this included their diminishing resources of tanks and assault guns. The *Panzerwaffe* were now duty-bound to improvise with what they had at their disposal and try to maintain themselves in the field, and so they hoped to wear down the enemy's offensive capacity. But in the south where the weight of the Soviet effort was directed, Army Group South's line began breaking and threatened to be ripped wide open. Stiff defensive action was now the stratagem placed upon the *Panzerwaffe*, but they lacked sufficient reinforcements and the strength of their armoured units dwindled steadily as they tried to hold back the Russian might.

During the first uneasy weeks of August 1943 the 1st Panzer Army and *Armee-abteilung* Kempf fought to hold ground along the Donets River whilst the final battle of Kharkov was fought out. Further north near the battered town of Akhtyrka the 4th Panzer Army was also fighting a frenzied battle of attrition. Along the whole Russian front massive Soviet artillery bombardments would sweep the German lines and inflict considerable casualties on both infantry and armoured vehicles. Throughout August and September the *Panzerwaffe* tried frantically to hold on to the receding front line. With just over 1,000 Panzers operating in southern Russia the Germans were seriously under strength and still further depleted by vehicles being constantly taken out for repair. Along many areas of the front, high losses resulted from inadequate supplies rather than the skill of the defenders.

In other areas of the Russian front the situation was just the same. Both Army Group Centre and Army Group North were trying desperately to hold the Soviets from breaking through their lines. Replacements continued to trickle through to help bolster the understrength *Panzerwaffe*. But in truth, the average new Panzer soldier, freshly recruited, was not as well trained as had been his predecessors during the early part of the campaign in Russia. Nevertheless, as with many Panzer men they were characterised, by high morale and a determination to do their duty.

In almost three months since the defeat at Kursk, Army Group Centre and South had been pushed back an average distance of 150 miles on a 650-mile front. Despite heavy resistance in many sectors of the front the Soviets lost no time in regaining as much territory as possible. In Army Group South where the front lines threatened to cave in completely under intense enemy pressure, frantic appeals to Hitler were made by Field Marshal Manstein for permission to withdraw his forces across the Dnieper River. What followed was a fighting withdrawal that degenerated into a race with the Russians for the river. Whilst the Panzer divisions covered the rear, the army group's columns withdrew on selected river crossing points at Cherkassy, Dniepropetrovsk, Kiev, Kanev and Kremenchuk, leaving behind a burnt a blasted wasteland during their retreat.

Kursk Order of Battle, July 1943

Army Group Centre (Günther von Kluge)

2nd Panzer Army (R. Schmidt)
XXXV Corps (Lothar Rendulic)
34th Infantry Division
56th Infantry Division
262nd Infantry Division
299th Infantry Division
LIII Corps (F. Gollwitzer)
208th Infantry Division
211th Infantry Division
293rd Infantry Division

25th Panzergrenadier Division
LV Corps (E. Jaschke)
110th Infantry Division
134th Infantry Division
296th Infantry Division
339th Infantry Division
Army Reserve
112th Infantry Division

9th Army (Walther Model)
XX Corps (R. von Roman)
45th Infantry Division
72nd Infantry Division
137th Infantry Division
251st Infantry Division
XLVI Panzer Corps (H. Zorn)
7th Infantry Division
31st Infantry Division
102nd Infantry Division
258th Infantry Division
XLI Panzer Corps (J. Harpe)
18th Panzer Division
86th Infantry Division
292nd Infantry Division

XLVII Panzer Corps (J. Lemelsen)
2nd Panzer Division
9th Panzer Division
20th Panzer Division
6th Infantry Division
XXIII Corps (J. Freissner)
216th Infantry Division
383rd Infantry Division
78th Assault Division
Army Reserve
4th Panzer Division
10th Panzergrenadier Division
12th Panzer Division

2nd Army (W. Weiss)

VII Corps (E.-E. Hell)
26th Infantry Division
68th Infantry Division
75th Infantry Division
88th Infantry Division
XIII Corps (E. Straube)
82nd Infantry Division
327th Infantry Division
340th Infantry Division
Army Group Reserve
5th Panzer Division
8th Panzer Division

Army Group South (Erich von Manstein)

4th Panzer Army (Hermann Hoth)

LII Corps (E. Ott)
57th Infantry Division
255th Infantry Division
332nd Infantry Division
XLVIII Panzer Corps (O. von Knobelsdorff)
3rd Panzer Division
11th Panzer Division
Panzergrenadier Division Grossdeutschland
167th Infantry Division
II SS Panzer Corps (P. Hausser)
1st SS Panzergrenadier Division Leibstandarte SS Adolf Hitler
2nd SS Panzergrenadier Division *Das Reich*
3rd SS Panzergrenadier Division *Totenkopf*

Army Group Kempf (W. Kempf)

III Panzer Corps (H. Breith)
6th Panzer Division
7th Panzer Division
19th Panzer Division
168th Infantry Division
Raus' Corps (E. Raus)
106th Infantry Division
320th Infantry Division
XLII Corps (F. Mattenklott)
39th Infantry Division
161st Infantry Division
282nd Infantry Division

Army Group Reserve
XXIV Panzer Corps (W. Nehring)
5th SS Panzergrenadier Division Wiking
17th Panzer Division

Luftwaffe
Luftflotte 4 (4th Air Fleet)
VIII Air Corps
Luftflotte 6
1st Air Division

Red Army

Western Front (V. Sokolovsky)

50th Army (I. Boldin)
38th Rifle Corps
17th Rifle Division
326th Rifle Division
413th Rifle Division

49th Rifle Division
64th Rifle Division
212th Rifle Division
324th Rifle Division

11th Guards Army (I. Bagramjan)
8th Guards Rifle Corps
11th Guards Rifle Division
26th Guards Rifle Division
83rd Guards Rifle Division
16th Guards Rifle Corps
1st Guards Rifle Division
16th Guards Rifle Division
31st Guards Rifle Division

169th Rifle Division
36th Guards Rifle Corps
5th Guards Rifle Division
18th Guards Rifle Division
84st Guards Rifle Division
108th Rifle Division
217th Rifle Division

1st Air Army (M. Gromov)
2nd Assault Air Corps
2nd Fighter Air Corps

8th Fighter Air Corps

Front assets
1st Independent Tank Corps

5th Independent Tank Corps

Bryansk Front (M. Popov)

3rd Army (A. Gorbatov)
41st Rifle Corps
235th Rifle Division
308th Rifle Division
380th Rifle Division

269th Rifle Division
283rd Rifle Division
342nd Rifle Division

61st Army (P. Belov)
9th Guards Rifle Corps
12th Guards Rifle Division
76th Guards Rifle Division
77th Guards Rifle Division
97th Rifle Division

110th Rifle Division
336th Rifle Division
356th Rifle Division
415th Rifle Division

63rd Army (V. Kolpakty)

5th Rifle Division
41st Rifle Division
129th Rifle Division
250th Rifle Division

287th Rifle Division
348th Rifle Division
397th Rifle Division

15th Air Army (N. Naumenko)

1st Guards Fighter Air Corps
3rd Assault Air Corps
25th Rifle Corps
186th Rifle Division

283rd Rifle Division
362nd Rifle Division
1st Independent Guards Tank Corps

Central Front (Konstantin Rokossovsky)

13th Army (N. Puchov)

17th Guards Rifle Corps
6th Guards Rifle Division
70th Guards Rifle Division
75th Guards Rifle Division
18th Guards Rifle Corps
2nd Airborne Guards Rifle Division
3rd Airborne Guards Rifle Division
4th Airborne Guards Rifle Division

15th Rifle Corps
8th Rifle Division
74th Rifle Division
148th Rifle Division
29th Rifle Corps
15th Rifle Division
81st Rifle Division
307th Rifle Division

48th Army (P. Romanenko)

42nd Rifle Corps
16th Rifle Division
202nd Rifle Division
399th Rifle Division

73rd Rifle Division
137th Rifle Division
143rd Rifle Division
170th Rifle Division

60th Army (I. Chernyakhovsky)

24th Rifle Corps
42nd Rifle Division
112th Rifle Division
30th Rifle Corps

121st Rifle Division
141st Rifle Division
322nd Rifle Division
Independent 55th Rifle Division

65th Army (P. Batov)

18th Rifle Corps
69th Rifle Division
149th Rifle Division
246th Rifle Division
27th Rifle Corps
60th Rifle Division

193rd Rifle Division
37th Guards Rifle Division
181st Rifle Division
194th Rifle Division
354th Rifle Division

70th Army (I. Galanin)
28th Rifle Corps
132nd Rifle Division
211th Rifle Division
280th Rifle Division
102nd Rifle Division

106th Rifle Division
140th Rifle Division
162nd Rifle Division
354th Rifle Division

2nd Tank Army (A. Rodin)
3rd Tank Corps

16th Tank Corps

16th Air Army (S. Rudenko)
3rd Bombing Air Corps
6th Mixed Air Corps
6th Fighter Air Corps

Independent 9th Tank Corps
Independent 19th Tank Corps

Voronezh Front (N. Vatutin)

6th Guards Army (I. Chistiakov)
22nd Guards Rifle Corps
67th Guards Rifle Division
71st Guards Rifle Division
90th Guards Rifle Division
23rd Guards Rifle Corps

51st Guards Rifle Division
52nd Guards Rifle Division
375th Rifle Division
Independent 89th Guards Rifle Division

7th Guards Army (M. Shumilov)
24th Guards Rifle Corps
15th Guards Rifle Division
36st Guards Rifle Division
72nd Guards Rifle Division
25th Guards Rifle Corps

73rd Guards Rifle Division
78th Guards Rifle Division
81st Guards Rifle Division
Independent 213th Rifle Division

38th Army (N. Chibisov)
50th Rifle Corps
167th Rifle Division
232nd Rifle Division
340th Rifle Division

51st Rifle Corps
180th Rifle Division
240th Rifle Division
Independent 204th Rifle Division

40th Army (K. Moskalenko)
47th Rifle Corps
161st Rifle Division
206th Rifle Division
237th Rifle Division
52nd Rifle Corps

100th Rifle Division
219th Rifle Division
309th Rifle Division
Independent 184th Rifle Division

69th Army (V. Kruchenkin)
48th Rifle Corps
107th Rifle Division
183rd Rifle Division
307th Rifle Division

49th Rifle Corps
111th Rifle Division
270th Rifle Division

1st Tank Army (M. Katukov)
6th Tank Corps
31st Tank Corps

3rd Mechanised Corps

2nd Air Army (S. Krasovskii)
1st Bombing Air Corps
1st Assault Air Corps
4th Fighter Air Corps
5th Fighter Air Corps
35th Guards Rifle Corps

92nd Guards Rifle Division
93rd Guards Rifle Division
94th Guards Rifle Division
Independent 2nd Guards Tank Corps
Independent 3rd Guards Tank Corps

Steppe Front (Ivan Konev)

5th Guards Army (A. Zhadov)
32nd Guards Rifle Corps
13th Guards Rifle Division
66th Guards Rifle Division
6th Airborne Guards Rifle Division
33rd Guards Rifle Corps

95th Guards Rifle Division
97th Guards Rifle Division
9th Airborne Guards Rifle Division
Independent 42nd Guards Rifle Division
Independent 10th Tank Corps

5th Guards Tank Army (Pavel Rotmistrov)
5th Guards Mechanised Corps

29th Tank Corps

5th Air Army (S. Gorunov)
7th Mixed Air Corps
8th Mixed Air Corps

3rd Fighter Air Corps
7th Fighter Air Corps

Panzer-Divisions, Kursk, July 1943

Panzer Divisions that participated in the battle of Kursk in July 1943:

2.Panzer-Division

Formed: Wurzburg, October 1935.

Divisional Insignia: For the invasion of Russia the division used a new inverted 'Y' with one mark. This was used during the first two years of the campaign in Russia. During mid-1943 a white trident sign replaced this emblem. The trident was used for the remainder of the war.

Units: Panzergrenadier Regiment 2, 304; Panzer Regiment 3; Panzer artillery Regiment 74; Panzer Aufkl Abt (Reconnaissance) 2.

Theatres of Operation: Army Group Centre (Smolensk, Orel, Kiev, Kursk) 1942–1943; France and Germany 1944–1945.

3.Panzer-Division

Formed: Berlin, October 1935.

Divisional Insignia: For the invasion of Russia a new sign was introduced and was regarded as the official sign. It was an inverted yellow 'Y' with two marks. In spite of the new sign, units of the division could use the bear in a white shield, and the tanks in Panzer-Regiment.6 also used the standing bear without a shield. The bear was often painted in various colours that included, white, yellow, blue and red. In 1943 Panzer-Regiment.6 adopted a regimental emblem that comprised of a black shield that was round on the bottom and flat on top, with the 1939–1940 divisional sign of the 4.Panzer-Division, and a pair of crossed swords below this.

Units: Panzergrenadier Regiments 3, 394; Panzer Regiment 6; Panzer Artillery Regiment 75; Panzer Aufkl Abt 3.

Theatres of Operation: Central Russia 1941–1942; Kursk, Kharkov, Dnepr Bend 1943; Ukraine and Poland 1944; Hungary and Austria 1944–1945.

4.Panzer-Division

Formed: Wurzburg, November 1938.

Divisional Insignia: In 1941 for the Russian campaign the division used the inverted 'Y' with three marks, and used this for the remainder of the war.

Units: Panzergrenadier Regiment 12, 33; Panzer Regiment 35; Panzer Artillery Regiment 103; Panzer Aufkl Abt 4.

Theatres of Operation: Central Russia – Caucasus 1942, Kursk 1943 and Latvia 1944; Germany 1945.

5.Panzer-Division

Formed: Oppeln, November 1939.

Divisional Insignia: On the Eastern Front Panzer-Regiment.31 adopted the red devil's head as a regimental symbol. This emblem, together with the yellow 'X', was used until the end of the war.

Units: Panzergrenadier Regiments 13, 14; Panzer Regiment 31; Panzer Artillery Regiment 116; Panzer Aufkl Abt 5.

Theatres of Operation: Central Russia – Kursk, Dnepr, Latvia, and Kurland 1941–1944; East Prussia 1944–1945.

6.Panzer-Division

Formed: Wuppertal, October 1939.

Divisional Insignia: For Kursk it used the letter symbol 'X' in yellow.

Units: Panzergrenadier Regiment 4, 114; Panzer Regiment 11; Panzer Artillery Regiment 76; Panzer Aufkl Abt 6.

Theatres of Operation: Russia 1941–1944; Hungary and Austria 1944–1945.

7.Panzer-Division

Formed: Weimar, October 1939.

Divisional Insignia: For the Kursk operation the armoured vehicles had a yellow 'Y'. The division fought mercilessly in Russia and retained the yellow 'Y' until the end of the war.

Units: Panzergrenadier Regiments 6, 7; Panzer Regiment 25; Panzer Artillery Regiment 78; Panzer Aufkl Abt 7.

Theatres of Operation: Central Russia 1941; Refit in France 1942; Southern Russia 1942; Kharkov 1942; Kursk 1943; Baltic Coast and Prussia 1944–1945.

8.Panzer-Division

Formed: Berlin, October 1938.

Divisional Insignia: In Russia the division used a new sign, a yellow 'Y' with one yellow mark. It was used until the end of the war.

Units: Panzergrenadier Regiments 8, 28; Panzer Regiment 10; Panzer Artillery Regiment 80; Panzer Aufkl Abt 8.

Theatres of Operation: Southern Russia 1941; Central Russia 1942; Kursk 1943.

9.Panzer-Division

Formed: January 1940.

Divisional Insignia: The divisions sign during the Kursk operation was a yellow 'Y' with two tick marks. This was used until the end of the war.

Units: Panzer Regiment 33; Panzer Grenadier Regiment 10, 11; Panzer Artillery Regiment 102.

Theatres of Operation: Russia Army Group South Ukraine, 1941–1942; Kiev 1941; Bryansk 1942; Kursk 1943; Odessa, Dnieper 1943–1944.

11.Panzer-Division

Formed: August 1940 at Breslau.

Divisional Insignia: This division received the official sign of a yellow circle divided by a vertical bar. The division's personal emblem was a white-stenciled figure of a ghost brandishing a sword. Because of this emblem the division became known as the 'Ghost' division, and fought until the end of the war.

Units: Panzergrenadier Regiments 110, 111; Panzer Regiment 15; Panzer Artillery Regiment 119; Panzer Aufkl Abt 11.

Theatres of Operation: Russia 1941–1944 (Orel, Belgorod, Krivoi Rog and Korsun); Northern France 1944.

12.Panzer-Division

Formed: October 1940.

Divisional Insignia: Its symbol was a yellow circle divided into three equal segments by 'Y'. The division did not modify its insignia and it carried it through the rest of the war.

Units: Panzergrenadier Regiments 5, 25; Panzer Regiment 29; Panzer Artillery Regiment 2; Panzer Aufkl Abt 12.

Theatres of Operation: Russia Army Group Centre 1941–1944; Russia 1941 – Minsk and Smolensk; Leningrad 1942; Orel and Middle Dnepr 1943; Kurland 1945 (captured by the Red Army).

17.Panzer-Division

Formed: October 1940.

Divisional Insignia: This division's emblem was entirely seen on the Eastern Front and was applied with a yellow 'Y' with two bars across the shaft.

Units: Panzergrenadier Regiments 40, 63; Panzer Regiment 39; Panzer Artillery Regiment 27; Panzer Aufkl Abt 17.

Theatres of Operation: Russia (central and southern sectors) 1941–1945.

18.Panzer-Division

Formed: October 1940.

Divisional Insignia: The division's emblem was a yellow 'Y' with three bars across its shaft. Panzer-Brigad.8 had a special marking, but this was not a divisional emblem. It had a shield edged white, with a white skull and lines of water in white. The division was disbanded in 1943 and was reorganised as an artillery division, but continued using the same divisional sign.

Major Units: Panzergrenadier Regiments 52, 101; Panzer Regiment 18; Panzer Artillery Regiment 88; Panzer Aufkl Abt 8.

Theatres of Operation: Russia (central and southern sectors) 1941–1943.

19.Panzer-Division

Formed: October 1940.

Divisional Insignia: Because of the area where the division was formed it adopted a yellow wolf-trap insignia. This emblem was seen on Panzers primarily on the Eastern Front, but did serve in Poland, notably in the Warsaw uprising in August 1944.

Major Units: Panzergrenadier Regiments 73, 74; Panzer Regiment 27; Panzer Artillery Regiment 19; Panzer Aufkl Abt 19.

Theatres of Operation: Russia 1941–1944 (Central and Southern Sectors).

20.Panzer-Division

Formed: October 1940.

Divisional Insignia: Its symbol was a yellow 'E' on its side, arms down, identical to the early 3.Panzer-Division emblem. In late 1943 the division received a new divisional insignia, which was a yellow arrow breaking through a curved borderline.

Major Units: Panzergrenadier Regiments 59, 112; Panzer Regiment 21; Panzer Artillery Regiment 92; Panzer Aufkl Abt 20.

Theatres of Operations: Russia 1941–1944; Moscow 1941; Orel 1943; Rumania 1944; East Prussia 1944; Hungary 1944.

Waffen SS Order of Battle, Kursk 1943

II.SS-Panzerkorps – SS-Obergruppenführer Paul Hausser
I.SS-Panzergrenadier-Division Leibstandarte 'Adolf Hitler'

SS-Brigadeführer Wisch: I.SS-Panzer-Regiment, I.SS-Panzer Grenadier-Regiment, 2.SS-Panzergrenadier-Regiment, I.SS-Panzer-Artillerie-Regiment, I.SS-Panzer-Reconnaissance-Battaillon, I.SS-Panzer-Engineer-Battaillon, I.SS-Flak-Battaillon.

Strength: 106 tanks and 35 assault guns.

2.SS-Panzergrenadier-Division 'Das Reich'

SS-Grupppenführer Kruger: I.SS-Panzer-Regiment, 3.SS-Panzergrenadier-Regiment 'Deutschland', 4.SS-Panzergrenadier-Regiment Der Führer, 2.SS-Panzer-Artillerie-Regiment, 2.SS-Panzer-Reconnaissance-Battaillon, 2.SS-Flak-Battaillon, 2.SS-Panzer-Engineer-Battaillon, 2.SS-Flak-Battaillon

Strength: 145 tanks and 34 assault guns.

3.SS-Panzergrenadier-Division 'Totenkopf'

SS-Brigadeführer Priess: 3.SS-Panzer-Regiment, 5.SS-Panzergrenadier-Regiment 'Thule', 6.SS-Panzergrenadier-Regiment 'Theodor Eicke', 3.SS-Panzer-Artillerie-Regiment, 3.SS-Panzer-Reconnaissance-Battaillon, 3.SS-Flak-Battaillon, 3.SS-Panzer-Engineer-Battaillon, 3.SS-Flak-Battaillon.

Strength: 139 tanks and 35 assault guns

122.Artillerie-Command (Arko)

I.Feld-Howitzer-Detachment, 861.Artillerie-Regiment (mot); I.Feld-Howitzer-Detachment, 3.Battaillon, 818.Artillerie-Regiment (mot); 3.Smoke-Truppen; 55.Werfer-Regiment; I.Werfer-Lehr-Regiment; 680.Pioneer-Regiment; 627.Poineer-Battaillon (mot), 666.Pioneer-Battaillon (mot)

Strength: 390 tanks and 104 assault guns.

Armoured Crew Uniforms

Wearing their special black Panzer uniforms the *Panzertruppen* were very distinctive from the German soldier wearing his field-grey service uniform. The uniform was first issued to crews in 1934, and was the same design and colouring for all ranks of the Panzer arm, except for some of the rank insignia and national emblem worn by officers and Generals. The colour of the uniform was specially dyed in black purely to hide oil and other stains from the environment of working with the armoured vehicles. Across Europe and into Russia these black uniforms would symbolise a band of elite troops that spearheaded their armoured vehicles and gained the greatest fame, or notoriety, of being part of the once powerful *Panzerwaffe*.

The black Panzer uniform itself was made of high quality black wool, which was smooth and free of imperfections. The uniform comprised of a short black double-breasted jacket worn with loose fitting black trousers. The deeply double-breasted jacket was high waisted and was specially designed to allow the wearer to move around inside his often cramped vehicle with relative comfort. The trousers were designed to be loose also in order to enable the wearer plenty of movement.

The 1934 pattern Panzer jacket was only in production until it was replaced in 1936 by the second pattern. This pattern was very popular and remained in production throughout the war. It was very similar to that of the first pattern. It had the short double-breasted jacket, which was normally worn open at the neck, showing the mouse-grey shirt and black tie. But with this design it did not lack the provision for buttoning and hooking the collar closed for protection against weather.

On the jacket the shoulder straps, collar patches and around the death head skull were piped in rose pink *Waffenfarbe* material. The rose pink piping was worn by all ranks around the outer edge of the jacket collar, but this design was discontinued by 1942. However, members of the 24th Panzer-Division did not wear the rose pink piping, theirs were gold yellow. This colour piping was purely for commemorative wear, originally worn by the 1st Kavallerie-Division, and was the only cavalry division in the German Army to be converted to a fully-fledged Panzer division.

The German national emblem on the double-breasted Panzer jacket was very similar to that worn on the German service uniform. It was stitched on the right breast in heavy white cotton weave, but the quality and colour did vary according to rank. For instance, they were also manufactured in grey cotton yarn or in fine aluminum thread. For officers and Generals of the *Panzertruppen* they were normally heavily embroidered in heavy silver wire.

The jacket was specially designed in order to limit the number of buttons worn on the outside of the coat, except for two small black buttons positioned one above the other on the far right side of the chest. These were stitched into place to secure the left lapel when the jacket was closed up at the neck.

The trousers worn were identical for all ranks. There was no piping used on the outer seams of the trouser legs. Generals of the *Panzertruppen* did not wear the red stripe on the trousers, as they did with the German army service uniform. The trousers did have two side pockets with button down pocket flaps, a fob pocket and a hip pocket. The trousers were generally gathered around the tops of the short leather lace-up ankle boots.

The headgear worn by the Panzer crews in 1941 was the Panzer enlisted mans field cap or *Feldmütze* and was worn by all ranks. It was black and had the early type national emblem stitched in white on the front on the cap above a woven cockade, which was displayed in the national colours. The field cap had a pink soutache.

For the next three years of the war the Panzer arm extensively wore the Panzer field cap. However, in 1943, a new form of head dress was introduced, the *Einheitsfeldmütze*, or better known as the Panzer enlisted mans model 1943 field cap. The M1943 cap was issued in black, but when stocks run low troops were seen wearing field-grey field caps. Both colours of the design were worn universally among Panzer crews and the cap insignia only slightly differed between the various ranks. The field-grey German Army steel helmet was also issued to the *Panzertruppen* as part of their regulation uniform. Generally the steel helmet was not worn inside the cramped confines of a tank, except when crossing over rough terrain and normally when the crewmember was exposed under combat conditions outside his vehicle. Many crews, however, utilised their steel helmets as added armoured protection and attached them to the side of the tank's cupola, and to the rear of the vehicle.

Another item of headgear worn by the Panzer arm was the officer's service cap or *Schirmmütze*. Although this service cap was not technically an item designed for the Panzer arm, it was still none the less an integral part of the Panzer officer's uniform and was worn throughout the war.

The Panzer uniform remained a well-liked and very popular item of clothing and did not alter extensively during the war. However, in 1942 a special two-piece reed-green denim suit was issued to Panzer crews in areas of operations where the climate was considered warmer than normal theatres of combat. The new denim suit was hard wearing, light and easy to wash, and many crews were seen wearing the uniform during the summer months. The uniform was generally worn by armoured crews, maintenance, and even *Panzergrenadiers* who were operating with half-tracked vehicles, notably the *Sd.Kfz.251* series. This popular and practical garment was identical in cut to the special black Panzer uniform. It consisted of the normal insignia, including the national emblem, Panzer death head collar patches and shoulder straps.

Apart from the uniforms worn by the Panzer crews, a special uniform was introduced for both *Sturmartillerie* and *Panzerjäger* units. The uniform was specially designed primarily to be worn inside and away from their armoured vehicles, and for this reason designers had produced a garment that gave better camouflage qualities than the standard black Panzer uniform. The uniform worn by units of the *Panzerjäger* was made entirely from lightweight grey-green wool material. The cut was very similar to that of the black Panzer uniform. However, it did differ in respect of insignia and the collar patches.

The *Panzerjäger* uniform was a very practical garment and it was identical to the cut of the *Sturmartillerie* uniform, but with the exception of the colour. The uniform was made entirely of field-grey cloth, but again differed in respect to certain insignia. The collar patches consisted of the death's head emblems, which were stitched on patches of dark blue-green cloth and were edged with bright red *Waffenfarbe* piping. However, officers did not display the death head collar patches, but wore the field service collar patches instead. No piping on the collar patches were used either.

Like the summer two-piece reed-green Panzer denim suit worn by Panzer crews, both tank destroyer and self-propelled assault gun units also had their own working and summer uniforms, which were also produced in the same colour and material.

Apart from the basic issued items of clothing worn by crews of the Panzer, tank destroyer and self-propelled assault gun units, crews were also issued with various items of clothing to protect them against the harsh climates. By the winter of 1942/43 the German Army had developed a new revolutionary item of clothing for the armoured crews called the parka. The parka was a well-made item of clothing that was well-padded and kept crews warm. Initially the parka was first designed in field-grey with a reversible winter white. But by late 1943 a new modification was made by replacing the field-grey side with a camouflage pattern, either in green splinter or tan water. The coat was double-breasted with the interior set of buttons being fastened to provide additional protection.